A Succinct Vie Importance and Pra Forming a Ship Cana across the Isthmus of Panama

H. R. Hill

Alpha Editions

This edition published in 2024

ISBN : 9789364734936

Design and Setting By
Alpha Editions
www.alphaedis.com
Email - info@alphaedis.com

As per information held with us this book is in Public Domain.
This book is a reproduction of an important historical work. Alpha Editions uses the best technology to reproduce historical work in the same manner it was first published to preserve its original nature. Any marks or number seen are left intentionally to preserve its true form.

ADVERTISEMENT.

The following observations were thrown together as the result of communications with several gentlemen locally acquainted with the Isthmus of Panama, and who expressed to the writer their astonishment, that amidst the numerous undertakings, of more or less utility, which science has realised in our time, one so important to the whole commercial world, so easy of accomplishment, and so certain to be productive of ample remuneration to the undertakers, as a Ship Canal through that Isthmus, had not been taken up. The idle objection, that if practicable it would not have been left unattempted for the last three hundred years, they considered, would have no weight in an age in which we have seen accomplished works that in our fathers' time, nay, even within our own memory, it would have been considered madness to propose,—witness steam-navigation and railways. It is not twenty years since Dr. Lardner, the author of a popular work on the steam-engine, then supposed to be a most competent authority, declared in his lectures that the application of steam-navigation to the voyage across the Atlantic was a mere chimera. So it has been with railways. Would not any man who fifty, or even twenty years ago, had predicted that the journey from London to Exeter would be accomplished *in five hours*, have been deemed a fit tenant for Bedlam? To contend that because a great undertaking has remained unattempted for a long series of years, *therefore* it is impracticable, is to put a stop to all improvement. At the suggestion of the friends before referred to, the writer is induced to print the following pages, with the hope of drawing to the subject of which they treat the attention of the mercantile and shipping interests. If they awaken an interest in the subject in those quarters, they will not be thrown away, and he is fully convinced that the more the subject is examined the stronger will be the conviction of the practicability of the undertaking.

23, Throgmorton Street,
February, 1845.

A SUCCINCT VIEW, &c.

From the first discovery of the American continent down to the present time, a shorter passage from the North Atlantic to the Pacific ocean than the tedious and dangerous voyage round Cape Horn has been a desideratum in navigation. During the dominion of old Spain in the New World the colonial policy and principles of that jealous nation, to which Central America belonged, opposed insurmountable obstacles to any proposal for effecting this great object; but the emancipation of the Spanish Colonies, and the erection of independent States in their stead, has broken down the barrier which Spanish jealousy had erected. The rulers of these states are not devoid of discernment to perceive that the exclusion of European Nations from the shores of the Pacific would be productive of immense injury to themselves, and that by making their own territory the high-road to the countries which are becoming important marts for the commerce of Europe, they are bringing wealth to their own doors, and increasing their own political importance.

In this, as in most other cases, individual and general benefit go hand in hand; for it cannot be doubted that were such a communication between the two Oceans made through Central America, it would prove of incalculable utility to all nations engaged in maritime commerce,—and sooner or later it will unquestionably be opened. This would be the shortest route from Europe, North America, and the western coast of Africa to every part of the western coast of the New World, to Australia, New Zealand, the numerous islands of the Pacific and the eastern coast of Asia,[1] as will be seen by a glance at the outline map of the world on Mercator's projection annexed to this pamphlet. The advantage of a Canal of sufficient size to allow large vessels to proceed through the Isthmus is therefore obvious.

But by whom is this work to be undertaken? the question is certainly not a British one alone, although the British Trade would derive immense benefit from its solution: it is a question in which the whole commercial world is more or less interested.

There must be either a combination of governments formed to defray so much each of the expense, or the work must be accomplished by a Joint Stock Company of individuals, who will indemnify themselves for their outlay by levying tolls upon those who avail themselves of the communication. As to such a combination of governments, the difficulty of procuring a sufficient grant of public money opposes a great obstacle to the realization of any such project.

To private enterprize chiefly then it must be committed; yet it may reasonably be expected that such countenance and support as the governments of the principal maritime powers can give, will be readily yielded to any association that will undertake the work.

There are several considerations which point out the present as the most auspicious moment for attaining the object in view. The profound peace with which Europe and the whole civilized world is now blessed, the abundance of capital in the money market, the present low rate of interest, and the difficulty of finding investments, are all favorable to the raising of the necessary funds; the immense strides which science has made in overcoming natural difficulties, once deemed insuperable, add to the means of accomplishment, while the growing importance of British Colonies in and about New Zealand, the inevitable impulse that recent events must give to the China trade,[2] and the efforts of all maritime nations to make establishments in the Polynesian Islands will render the Canal a certain source of profit and honor to those who will aid in its formation.

Several parts of the Isthmus of America have been proposed for the communication between the two seas, such as the Province of Nicaragua, the Isthmus of Tehuantepec, &c.; but invincible obstacles occur in all those localities, while on the contrary the Isthmus of Panama is beyond doubt the most favorable point, according to the opinion of all the scientific and practical men who have visited that part of the new world.[3] We shall proceed, therefore, to describe that Isthmus as far as is necessary for the present purpose.

The Isthmus of Panama[4] may be considered as extending from the Meridian of 77° to that of 81° W. of Greenwich. Its breadth at the narrowest point, opposite to the city of Panama, is about thirty miles. The general feature of the Isthmus on the map is that of an arc, or bow, the chord of which lies nearly east and west. It now forms a province of the republic of New Granada.

It may appear strange, yet it is now well known to be the fact, that although the small width of the Isthmus was ascertained soon after the discovery of America, its natural features remained entirely unknown for three hundred years. Robertson, in his History of America, states that the Isthmus is traversed in all its length by a range of high mountains, and it was reserved for our scientific countryman, Lloyd, who surveyed the Isthmus in 1828 and 1829, by direction of Bolivar, then president of the Republic of Colombia, to dispel the illusion. From his observations, confirmed by more recent travellers, it is now ascertained that the chain of the Andes terminates near Porto Bello to the east of the Bay of Limon, otherwise called Navy Bay, and that the Isthmus is, in this part, throughout its whole width, a flat country. It was also long supposed that there was an enormous difference between the rise and fall of the tide in the Pacific and Atlantic Oceans on either side of the Isthmus, and that the opening of a communication between the two seas would be productive of danger to a large portion of the American continent. It is now, however, ascertained that the difference of altitude is very trifling, not more than thirteen feet at high water.[5] The prevalence of these errors may have tended, in combination with Spanish jealousy, unhealthiness of climate on the Atlantic side, the denseness of the forests, and the unsettled state of the Government for some years after the Spanish yoke was shaken off, to prevent the undertaking now proposed from being seriously considered.

Panama is the principal city on the Isthmus. Its site has been once changed. When the Spaniards first visited the Isthmus in 1512, the spot on which the old city was afterwards built, was already occupied by an Indian population, attracted by the abundance of fish on the coast, and who are said to have named it "Panama" from this circumstance, the word signifying much fish. They, however, were speedily dispossessed; and even so early as 1521, the title and privileges of a city were conferred on the Spanish town by the emperor, Charles the Fifth. In the year 1670, it was sacked and reduced to ashes by the buccaneer, Morgan, and was subsequently built where it now stands.

The position of the present town of Panama is in latitude 8° 57' N.; longitude 79° 30' W. of Greenwich, on a tongue of land, shaped nearly like a spear head, extending a considerable distance out to sea, and gradually swelling towards the middle. Its harbour is protected by a number of islands, a short distance from the main land, some of which are of considerable size, and highly cultivated.

There is good anchorage at each of these islands, and supplies of ordinary kinds, including excellent water, which may be obtained from several of them.[6]

The city of Panama was, in the 17th century, a place of great importance, but has gradually sunk into comparative insignificance. The policy of the present Government of New Granada is to restore this city to its pristine importance, and for this reason, one terminus of the intended Ship Canal should be at, or as near as conveniently may be to, this position.

The natural obstacles to be overcome in forming a Canal between Panama, and the *nearest point* of the opposite coast, which is the Gulph of San Blas (likewise called the Bay of Mandingo), render it expedient to select a position west of that line, and the happy coincidence of two navigable rivers, traversing the low lands to the west of Porto Bello, the one falling into the Atlantic, and the other into the Pacific Ocean, which may either form part of the navigation, or be used to feed the Canal, renders that part of the Isthmus the most eligible for this purpose. The rivers alluded to, are the Chagres and the Rio Grande.

The town of Chagres, at the mouth of the river of the same name, is about thirty-two miles west of Porto Bello (Puerto Velo); it is situated on the north bank of the river, which falls into the Caribbean Sea. The harbour formed by the mouth of the river having been greatly neglected, has been much choked up; but it would be unnecessary to incur the expense of improving it, for Navy Bay, called also the Bay of Limon, lying immediately to the eastward of Chagres, is a large and spacious harbour, being three miles wide at the mouth, and having sufficient draught of water for the largest ships in the British Navy. The river Chagres approaches within three miles of the head of this Bay; the ground between is a dead level,[7] and all writers agree that, the difficulties of the harbour being surmounted, there is abundance of water in the Chagres. It is, therefore, proposed either to cut a Canal from Navy Bay to the Chagres, and then to ascend that river as far as its junction with the river Trinidad, and after traversing a part of the latter, to construct a canal which shall connect the Trinidad with the River Farfan, a branch of the Rio Grande, and to proceed by that river to Panama; or should the Bay of Chorrera, which is laid down in the plan, be deemed a preferable harbour, to branch off to that bay; or to make the Canal across the whole width of the isthmus, from the Bay of Limon to that of Panama, using the rivers Trinidad, Farfan, and Bernardino, and other streams which cross the line, for the supply of the Canal.

The plan annexed to this pamphlet will exhibit the two lines, and the reader will perceive that a small Lake, called the Lake of Vino Tinto, may, if the first proposal is adopted, be made available, and so lessen the extent of the Canal. If the Rivers are used as a part of the Navigation, the distance between that point of the River Trinidad at which the Canal would commence, as shewn in the plan, and the point where the Farfan ceases to be navigable, is only 25 miles, and there is no high land intervening, the chain of the Andes terminating several miles to the eastward of the valley of the Chagres, as before mentioned. If the other plan be adopted, the length of the Canal will be 58 miles.

Although at first sight it may appear to be a work of supererogation, to carry the Canal over that part of the Isthmus which is traversed by navigable rivers, it is by many engineers considered preferable in forming a Canal, to use the rivers in its vicinity only for the purpose of supplying the Canal with water, and not as a continuation of the inland navigation, on account of the variation in the depth of rivers from floods, or other accidents. Which of these two courses would be most expedient in the present instance, may be safely left to the determination of the engineer selected to carry out the undertaking;—it is sufficient to know that *either is practicable*, and that the expense of cutting the Canal the whole width of the isthmus would meet with a corresponding return to the undertakers.

The principal difficulty anticipated in the execution of the work, arises from the unhealthiness of the climate on the Atlantic side of the isthmus—a difficulty to which the writer is by no means insensible. It has, however, been exaggerated, and by proper arrangements may be surmounted. The causes of this unhealthiness are chiefly the swampy state of the ground on the Atlantic side of the Isthmus (which the Canal itself, acting as a drain upon the surrounding country, will greatly tend to remove), and the malaria engendered by the closeness of the woods, and by the accumulation of decayed vegetable substances, which the opening of the country, incidental to the formation of the Canal now proposed, and the road afterwards adverted to, will tend to alleviate; and after all, those who have visited this part of the Isthmus, concur in stating that the mortality in the low lands about Chagres is principally owing to the imprudence of the Europeans visiting the country, in exposing themselves to the night dews by sleeping in the open air, and indulging in habits of intemperance.[8] If an association were formed for carrying out the work now projected, one of the first cares of the managers should be to erect huts or barracks for the protection of the workmen against exposure to the weather, and the appointment of a medical officer, who should be entrusted with sufficient powers to ensure obedience to his regulations.

If the industry of the native population could be depended upon, there would be no want of labourers inured to the climate, but the inertness of the natives renders it inexpedient to rely upon them alone; although, working in conjunction with Europeans, and stimulated by their example, and by the love of gain, their services may, no doubt, be made available. There is, however, no difficulty in collecting from the Southern States of North America a sufficient number of Irish labourers inured to a tropical climate, as was lately clearly shewn by the formation of a railway at the Havanna, which was almost entirely constructed by this class of men.

Any deficiency of labourers, it is considered, could easily be drawn from the mining districts of Cornwall, from Ireland itself, or from Scotland, or the North of England.

The next consideration is the expense of constructing a Ship Canal across the Isthmus, and the probable returns. The estimates which have been made, and of which the result is given below, suppose the Canal to be cut through the whole width of the Isthmus, from the Bay of Limon to that of Chorrera, and they include a large outlay for improving the harbours formed by the two bays.

The first item that would occur in an undertaking of the same nature *in this country*, would be the purchase of the land. Here a great advantage presents itself in the present enterprise; for the Government of New Granada, fully appreciating the permanent advantages to be derived to the state from the execution of a work, which it is unequal to accomplish by its own resources, has repeatedly offered to grant the land required, for 60, 70, or 80 years, according to the magnitude of the works, free of rent, or burdens of any kind, and to admit the importation, free of duty, of all materials and provisions necessary for the undertaking.

EXPENSES.

The expenses of cutting the Canal, and of the direction and management of a Company constituted for that purpose, up to the period of the opening of the Canal have been estimated at[9]	£1,713,177
But if it be deemed expedient to raise two millions, in order to provide for any unforseen casualties, the difference will be	286,823
Total outlay	£2,000,000

RETURNS.

From information derived from official sources in England, France, and the United States of America, it is estimated that the tonnage of vessels belonging to those countries and to Holland, trading in countries to which the Canal through the Isthmus will be the shortest voyage, amount to 799,427 tons per annum; and there can be no doubt that the opening of the Canal would create a great extension of trade to the South Seas, as well as induce the owners of many of the vessels now using the navigation by the Cape of Good Hope to prefer the shorter voyage through the Isthmus; and when we add to this consideration, the fact that the above calculations do not include the vessels belonging to Spain, Sardinia, the Hanse Towns, and other nations of minor importance as maritime powers, but possessing in the aggregate a trade not altogether inconsiderable, nor the traffic that may be expected to flow to the Pacific from the West Indies, the British Colonies in North America, and the countries on the north east coast of South America, the tonnage of vessels that will be attracted to the Canal may be fairly estimated at 800,000 tons.

A tonnage duty of $2 per ton, on 800,000 tons will produce $1,600,000, equal, at 4s. 2d., to	£333,333
Allowing a deduction for the annual expenses of a sum much larger than will probably be required, say	40,000
There will remain a Balance of annual profit of	£293,333

This in turn will give upwards of 14½ per cent. profit on the above outlay of £2,000,000.

The Isthmus has recently been surveyed by M. Garella, an eminent French Engineer, whose opinions will be found in the extract from the *Moniteur*, contained in the Appendix. He was employed to make the survey by the French Government, and his official Report has not yet been made public. He differs in several material points from M. Morel, another French gentleman, who is stated to have lately surveyed the Isthmus;[10] but if the formation of a canal should be undertaken by an English company, the parties engaged in the enterprize would doubtless be guided by the English engineer whom they would employ, in the selection of the most eligible line, while the labours of his predecessors would greatly aid him in his survey.

As subservient to the grand project of a Ship Canal, an improved road across the Isthmus has been projected. The abundance of hard wood to be found on the spot, would furnish a cheap material for converting it into a tram-road. The expense has been estimated by French engineers at £40,000 sterling, and the returns, even according to the present transit of goods and passengers across the Isthmus by the miserable road now existing from Cruces to Panama, would, at a very moderate toll, be enormous on that outlay.

APPENDIX.

The following Extracts from Authors who have treated of the Isthmus of Panama will tend to illustrate the subject of the foregoing pages.

Dampier, (1681).

"Panama enjoys a good air, lying open to the sea-wind. There are no woods nor marshes near Panama, but a brave dry champaign land, not subject to fogs nor mists."

Humboldt, (1803).

"It appears that we find a prolongation of the Andes towards the South Sea, between Cruces and Panama. However, Lionel Wafer assures us that the hills which form the central chain, are separated from one another by valleys, which allow free course for passage of the rivers; if this last assertion be founded, we might believe in the possibility of a canal from Cruces to Panama, of which the navigation would only be interrupted by a very few locks."

The Edinburgh Review, for Jan. 1809, Art. II. page 282.

"In enumerating, however, the advantages of a commercial nature which would assuredly spring from the emancipation of South America, we have not yet noticed the greatest, perhaps, of all,—the mightiest event probably in favor of the peaceful intercourse of nations which the physical circumstances of the globe present to the enterprise of man,—we mean the formation of a navigable passage across the Isthmus of Panama, the junction of the Atlantic and Pacific Oceans. It is remarkable that this magnificent undertaking, pregnant with consequences so important to mankind, and about which so little is known in this country, is so far from being a romantic or chimerical project, that, it is not only practicable but easy. The River Chagres, which falls into the Atlantic at the town of the same name, about 18 leagues to the westward of Porto Bello is navigable as far as Cruces, within five leagues of Panama; but though the formation of a Canal from this place to Panama, facilitated by the valleys through which the present road passes, appears to present no very formidable obstacles, there is still a better expedient. At the distance of about five leagues from the mouth of the Chagres it receives the river Trinidad, which is navigable to Embarcadero; and from that place to Panama is a distance of about 30 miles, through a level country, with a fine river,[11] to supply water for the Canal, and no difficulty whatever to counteract the noble undertaking. The ground has been surveyed, and not the practicability only, but the facility of the work completely ascertained. In the next place, the important requisite of safe harbours, at the two extremities of a Canal, is here supplied to the extent of our utmost wishes. At the mouth of the Chagres is a fine Bay, which received the British 74 gun-ships in 1740, and at the other extremity is the famous harbour of Panama."

J. A. Lloyd, F. R. S.

"It is generally supposed in Europe that the great chain of mountains, which in South America forms the Andes, and in North America the Mexican and Rocky Mountains, continues nearly unbroken through the Isthmus. This, however, is not the case: the Northern Cordillera breaks into detached mountains on the eastern side of the province of Veragua. These are of considerable height, extremely abrupt and rugged, and frequently exhibit an almost perpendicular face of bare rock. To these succeed numerous conical mountains rising out of Savannahs and plains, and seldom exceeding from 300 to 500 feet in height. Finally between Chagres on the Atlantic side, and Chorrera on the Pacific side, the conical mountains are not so numerous, having plains of great extent interspersed, with occasional insulated ranges of hills of inconsiderable height and extent. From this description it will be seen that the spot where the continent of America is reduced to nearly its narrowest limits, is also distinguished by a break for a few miles of the Great chain of Mountains, which otherwise extends, with but few exceptions, to its extreme northern and southern limits. *This combination of circumstances points out the peculiar fitness of the Isthmus of Panama for the establishment of a communication across.*"

Philosophical Transactions, 1830, Part I., p. 65.

"Should a time arrive when a project of a water communication across the Isthmus may be entertained, the river Trinidad will probably appear the most favourable route. The river is for some distance both broad and deep. Its banks are also well suited for wharfs."

Philosophical Transactions, ibid, p. 66.

"The river, its channel, and the banks, which, in the dry season, embarrass its navigation, are laid down in the manuscript plan with great care and minuteness. It is subject to one great inconvenience, that vessels drawing more than 12 feet water, cannot enter the river, even in perfectly calm weather, on account of a stratum of slaty limestone, which runs at a depth at high water of fifteen feet, from a point on the main land to some rocks in the middle of the entrance of the harbour, and which are just even with the water's edge; which, together with the lee current that sets on the southern shore, particularly in the rainy season, renders the entrance extremely difficult and dangerous....

"The value of the Chagres, considered as the port of entrance for all communications, whether by the river Chagres, Trinidad, or by railroads across the plains, is greatly limited from the above mentioned cause. It would prove in all cases a serious disqualification, *were it not one which admits of a simple and effectual remedy, arising from the proximity of the Bay of Limon*, otherwise called Navy Bay, with which the river might easily be connected. The coves of this bay afford excellent and secure anchorage in its present state, and the whole harbour is capable of being rendered, by obvious and not very expensive means, one of the most commodious and safe harbours in the world.

"By the good offices of H. M. Consul in Panama,[12] and the kindness of the Commander of H. M. Ship Victor, I obtained the use of that ship and her boats in making the accompanying plan of this bay.... The soundings were taken by myself, with the assistance of the master. It will be seen from this plan, that the distance from one of the best coves (in respect to anchorage), across the separating country from the Chagres, and in the most convenient track, is something less than three miles to a point in the river about three miles from its mouth. I have traversed the intervening land which is particularly level, and in all respects suitable for a canal, which, being required for so short a distance, might well be of sufficient depth to admit vessels of any reasonable draft of water, and would obviate the inconvenience of the shallow water at the entrance of the Chagres."

Ibid, p. 68.

Extract from the Moniteur Parisien of Monday, October 14, 1844.

"Some of the public papers in announcing the return of M. Garella to Paris, have asserted that the surveys made by that Engineer on the Isthmus of Panama have led him to conclude that the formation of a canal in that Country which should unite the two oceans is impossible. This assertion is completely erroneous. The Report that this Engineer intends to lay before the Ministers is not yet completed; but the principal results of his voyage are already known, and which far from having established the impossibility of the execution of the projected work, prove on the contrary that the soil of this portion of the Isthmus is not such as to threaten any serious obstruction to the performance of a work of the kind.

"The line which has been explored by M. Garella, seems to be about 76 kilometres (46½ miles) in length. Its point of termination upon the side of the Atlantic is in the Bay of Limon (Puerto de Naos) situated a little east of the mouth of the Rio Chagres, and already indicated five years ago by Mr. Lloyd, where there is a depth of water of 10 metres (35 ft. 5 in.), and where it will be easy to form an excellent port at a small expense. By this means may be avoided the village of Chagres, situated at the month of the river of that name, but of which the real unhealthiness has been so much exaggerated, as to create an unfounded alarm among too many travellers. On the Pacific Ocean the Canal should terminate at a little bay named Ensenada de Voca de Monte, situated between Panama and the mouth of the Caimito, where there is four metres (13 ft. 1 in.) depth of water at low tide, which, with 3 metres 20 centimetres (10½ ft.), which represent the difference at high tide, gives a sufficient depth of water for the largest merchant ships.

"The rigidly exact levellings which have been taken by M. Garella, establish that the mean level of the Pacific Ocean is two metres 80 centimetres (9 ft. 2 in.) higher than that of the Atlantic, and that the minimum point of the chain to overcome, which will be the most elevated point of the line of the work, is 120 metres (131 yards[13]) above the height of the sea at Panama. The surveys which have been made, prove at the same time that the height may be reduced to 90 metres (90 yards and a half) by a trench from four to five kilometres (between two and three miles) in length, which, although considerable, has nothing discouraging, considering the powers which science puts at the disposal of the engineer. This height will render it necessary to form 30 locks at each of the declivities.

"M. Garella is convinced, as much by his own observations, as by the information that he has been able to obtain upon the spot, that all that has been said of the unhealthiness of the Isthmus has been exaggerated. Panama is, of all the towns upon the coast of America which are situated between the Tropics, the most healthy, and perhaps the only town where the yellow fever has never appeared. The interior of the Isthmus, through which water courses find a rapid passage, is equally healthy, and is inhabited by a robust and hospitable population, which, although thinly spread over a large tract of country, as in almost all the countries of Central and South America, together with that of the neighbouring countries, may amply supply the labourers necessary for the work, in case of its execution. Chagres is the only point where the climate has any degree of unhealthiness, owing to pure local circumstances; but this point will be avoided by the line contemplated by M. Garella. Then in the unhealthiness of the climate there is nothing to be dreaded for such artizans as masons and carpenters, whom it would be necessary to send out from Europe.

"On the other hand the soil is of wonderful fertility. The cattle, far from being scarce in that part are, on the contrary, abundant, especially in the Canton of Chiriqui, on the Pacific Ocean, a little to the west of Panama. There will, therefore, be easily found within the country the means of provisioning a large number of workmen.

"The exact estimate of the expense attending the formation of a Canal at Panama cannot be known until the report of M. Garella shall be completed. But the foregoing explanations are of sufficient weight, as a decided result of his surveys, to enable us to see that, against the undeniable utility of a Canal that should be of sufficient dimensions to allow the passage of the largest merchants' ships, we can hardly place in the balance the consideration of any expenses whatsoever, nor question the long series and increasing importance of the advantages which must arise from it."

By way of summary: the opinion of this engineer on the possibility of the formation of the Canal in question, is contained in the following lines of a letter addressed by him to the Governor of Panama, dated the 7th July, 1844, and a few days before his departure from that country, translated from the "*Cartilla Popular*," a public paper published at Panama, and written in Spanish.

"I am nevertheless partly able to satisfy your just and natural impatience, in announcing to you that a Canal across the Isthmus between the river Chagres, and a point of the coast of the Pacific Ocean, in the environs of Panama, is a work of very possible execution, and even easier than that of many Canals which have been formed in Europe."

M. Morel.

The author has been furnished with the following summary of the opinions of M. Morel, who has been a resident for some years at Panama. M. Morel is stated to have surveyed the whole line of country destined to be appropriated to a road, as well as the ground through which a Canal might be opened, and as the result of his surveys and observations, he is reported to state—

1. That the width of the Isthmus of Panama, in *a direct line*, does not exceed 33 miles.

2. That the chain of mountains which incloses the country terminates precisely between Chagres and Panama, and forms a valley, which is crossed in all directions by numerous streams.

3. That besides those streams, four rivers of more importance, the Chagres and Trinidad, which flow into the Atlantic, and the Farfan and Rio Grande, which discharge themselves into the Pacific, in the immediate vicinity of Panama, can be made available.

4. That the soundings of the River Chagres show its depth to be from $16\frac{1}{2}$ to 22 feet, to its junction with the river Trinidad, the tide being felt for four miles up the last named river. The breadth of the Chagres is 220 feet from its mouth to the Trinidad.

5. That it becomes only necessary to unite these rivers by a Canal, the length of which would not exceed 25 miles, and which would be abundantly supplied by the numerous streams already mentioned.

6. That the land through which this Canal is to pass, is almost on a level with the sea, the highest point being 36 feet, thus presenting none of those serious difficulties which generally attend a work of this description.[14]

7. That the country abounds with the necessary materials for building, such as free-stone, clay, lime, and wood.

8. That there can exist no fear of a scarcity of labourers and workmen, from the number who have already been enrolled by the government of New Granada, which amounts to 4000 and upwards.

9. That the objection which has often been started against the possibility of forming a water communication across the Isthmus of Panama, founded on the difference supposed to exist between the levels of the two seas, is totally at variance with the natural state of things, the tides rising to different heights at Chagres and at Panama, thus placing the Pacific sometimes above, and sometimes below the Atlantic.

Lastly, M. Morel remarks, that Baron de Humboldt, the celebrated Geographer, M. Arago, the eminent Astronomer, F.R.S., and Commander Garnier, of the French Brig of War, "Le Laurier," have proved that if there be any inequality of height, the average difference of level cannot exceed one metre (about one yard English).

POSTSCRIPT.

Since the foregoing pamphlet was in print, an Article has appeared in the Morning Chronicle of the 16th May, 1845, in which it is alleged, upon the authority of an Article in the *Journal des Debats*, that M. Garella has given in his Report to the French Government, and that he reports in favour of the practicability of the scheme, but that he found the lowest elevation between the two oceans to amount to, from 120 to 160 metres, and that this being, as he says, too great an elevation for a Ship Canal, he proposes an enormous Tunnel capable of allowing Frigates to pass through—that he thinks from examination of the soil, that a Tunnel of 100 feet in height above the surface of the Canal will be practicable, and might be made with a reasonable outlay of money; and that the length of the Tunnel would be 5,350 metres, and the expense of it about 44 millions of francs (£1,760,000).

It is impossible to read this statement without feeling a strong suspicion that, for some object which does not appear, it is the wish of the French Government, or those who have put the statement forth, to deter others from embarking in the formation of a Canal across the Isthmus of Panama; for the recommendation of a Tunnel of 5,350 metres (about three miles) in length, and 100 feet in height, is not only preposterous in itself, as applied to a Ship Canal, but is wholly at variance with M. Garella's own letter to the Governor of Panama (ante p. 26), and with the statement of his opinions in the Article in the *Moniteur Parisien* (ante p. 23), which Article is believed to have been written by himself. It is true that M. Garella, being a Mining Engineer (*Ingénieur des Mines*) may have a partiality for subterraneous works; and this refection provokes the observation, that it is singular that the French Government should have selected, for this very important survey, an Engineer of Mines (however eminent in his department), rather than one experienced in the formation of Canals, when it had so many of the latter at command.

It is difficult to conceive that the writer of the letter to the Governor of Panama, and of the Article in the *Moniteur Parisien* can be sincere in recommending a Tunnel; and the conclusion is irresistible, that if the Article in the *Debats* has any foundation in the forthcoming Report, it is a stroke of policy on the part of the French Government, to discourage an undertaking which its own subjects have not sufficient enterprize to accomplish, and which it would object to see executed by other nations.

In the present state of the question, it may not be immaterial to remark, that on a comparison lately made by an English Engineer of Mr. Lloyd's levels, with the survey alleged to have been made by M. Morel (the accuracy of which is necessarily impugned by M. Garella, if he asserts that an elevation of 120 metres must be overcome), it appears that the levels ascribed to M. Morel, very nearly agree with those of Mr. Lloyd, and are substantially corroborated by his survey.

FOOTNOTES:

[1] The reader will remember that to discover a more direct passage to India than the voyage round Africa, which the Portuguese were then exploring, was the object of Columbus' voyage which led to the discovery of America, and the present proposal is to realize the project of that great navigator. The name of "Indies" was given to his discoveries, under a belief that he had actually reached India, a name still preserved in our "West Indies."—*Robertson's America*, book ii., vol. i, pp. 70 and 124-5, (edit. of 1821). It may well excite astonishment that more than three centuries should have been allowed to elapse before the full accomplishment of this great man's undertaking.

[2] The intelligent observer of passing events will not fail to see in the "signs of the times" indications that the day is not far distant when the important Empire of Japan will follow the example of China, and throw open its harbours to European commerce—a consummation devoutly to be wished—and which the present expedition to those shores, under the command of Sir Edward Belcher, is likely to accelerate.

A more immediate development of commercial enterprise cannot fail to result from the opening of a Ship Canal through the Isthmus of Panama; viz., *a direct trade* between the West India Islands, English, French, and Spanish, and the countries which have been named. From this consideration, the West India proprietors and merchants, whose property in those colonies has been of late years so much depreciated, are deeply interested in the success of this undertaking.

[3] The opinions of writers who have visited the locality, will be found in the Appendix. To those of Mr. Lloyd, who was sent by Bolivar to survey the Isthmus in 1827, in particular, great weight is due.

[4] It was formerly called the Isthmus of Darien, but that name has fallen into disuse among all persons who have any intercourse with that part of the globe, though still preserved in some of the atlases.

[5] J. A. Lloyd, F. R. S., Philosophical Transactions of the Royal Society of London, 1830, Part I. pp. 62, 63.

[6] J. A. Lloyd, F. R. S., Geographical Society's Transactions, vol. I.

[7] J. A. Lloyd. See Appendix.

[8] The writer has conferred with several gentlemen who have visited the Isthmus, and who agree in this opinion.

[9] It may be here stated that the Caledonian Canal, and the Canal from Amsterdam to Niewdiep, the two most expensive Ship Canals which have been made in Europe (and which approximate in magnitude the Canal now projected), were formed at a much less expense per mile than has been allowed in this estimate.

[10] See Appendix, page 26.

[11] Probably the Farfan.

[12] Malcolm MacGregor, Esq.

[13] The Canal of Languedoc is at its highest point 600 feet above the level of the sea.—*M'Culloch's Commercial Dict., Art. Canals.*

[14] It may be possible to reconcile the apparent contradiction between the fact here stated by M. Morel, and the report of M. Garella, by mentioning that the latter suggests the propriety of carrying the Canal over a hill 120 yards high, and thus shortening its length, rather than to adopt M. Morel's line of survey along the flat and low lands, which is the longest of the two.

THE END.